How To
Continuously
Improve
The Quality Of Customer Service
At
Golf And Country Clubs

by
Andrew R. Cornesky
&
Robert A. Cornesky

CORNESKY & ASSOCIATES, INC.
489 Oakland Park Blvd.
Port Orange, Florida 32127
Phone: (800) 388-8682 or (904) 760-5866
Fax: (904) 756-6755

E-Mail: TQM1BOB@AOL.COM

TABLE OF CONTENTS

Page

Introduction 1
    Purpose of this booklet................................2
    What is Continuous Quality Improvement
      (CQI)..2
    How are golf and country clubs different? 3
    Why must we improve the systems of
      golf and country clubs? 3
    The six steps for implementing CQI 4

Chapter One:
Educate the Management 7
    Topic 1:   Approaches to CQI..........................9
    Topic 2:   Principles of CQI............................9
    Topic 3:   Applying the Malcolm Baldrige
                   Criteria to Measure Quality.........10
    Topic 4:   The Plan-Do-Check-Act Cycle......11
    Topic 5:   CQI Tools and Techniques............12

Chapter Two:
Establish Commitment of the Management 15
    Make it apparent that CQI is not being tested
      as a concept 16
    Appoint a Coordinator for CQI 17
    Appoint a CQI community advisory
      council 21
    Appoint a CQI advisory council for each
      unit/department..22

Encourage members of the governing board to
 undergo CQI training 24
Have a management team write a quality
 philosophy guide book 25
Make quality improvement an agenda item at
 performance evaluations 26
Establish and measure quality goals 27

Chapter Three:
Establish Quality Awareness 29
 Educate the employees 30
 Establish quality councils 32
 Establish quality improvement teams 33

Chapter Four:
Establish Baseline Data 45
 Involve everyone and keep it simple 50
 Get training on Malcolm Baldrige National ......
 Quality Award Criteria 51
 Establish an accounting procedure 52
 Collect and plot cost of nonconformance
 data 53

Chapter Five:
Set Goals 55

Chapter Six:
Establish a Recognition Program 59

Suggested Readings 63

INTRODUCTION

As a golf or country club manager, you are always looking for ways to improve your services, cut costs and yet maintain your high standards. As consultants, we have devoted many years to helping managers like you achieve those goals by understanding and applying Continuous Quality Improvement (CQI) ideas. While CQI was born in manufacturing, it is not restricted to behind factory walls. We bring to your attention those steps that you might want to consider to help you apply basic CQI principles to your golf or country club.

The process borrows extensively from recognized leaders in the quality field and encourages you to develop your own quality improvement model based on your club's particular mission.

Using CQI procedures, you and your colleagues will constantly examine how things are being done and look for ways to improve the processes and systems. That effort will evolve into better service that leads to increased customer satisfaction and reduced costs.

**Good is not good
where better
is expected.
Thomas Fuller**

Purpose of this book
This book explains CQI and recommends that six steps be considered before implementing CQI at any golf or country club.

What is CQI?
CQI is a philosophy that encourages everyone in your club to know its mission and to adopt quality-driven procedures that continuously improve on how the work is done in order to increase customer satisfaction. The general principles of CQI encourages all employees—from the CEO to grounds crew—to point out processes and systems that are not working properly and to recommend improvements. CQI encourages teamwork and shuns inflexible rules and regulations.

Honest differences are often a healthy sign of progress.
Mahatma Gandhi

How are golf and country clubs different?

Most people associated with golf and country clubs would agree that the internal organization of most clubs does not resemble that of a hotel or bank, both of which provide services. Golf and country clubs are different. They are different in institutional setting, in purpose, in operation, and hence in internal organization.

Why must we improve the systems of golf and country clubs?

You are probably wondering why golf and country clubs should consider CQI at all. Doesn't the United States enjoy the best golfing system in the world? It certainly has enabled our country to become the world leader in golf and to maintain that position.

The United States has the best golf courses in the world. Most people would agree that our system of private and public courses is the best, however, the number of courses is increasing and the battle for customers is at an all time high. Those clubs that can reduce costs while they exceed the expectations of their customers will be successful. Those that do not, will falter. CQI remains the best method for boosting customer satisfaction and quality service

The six steps for implementing CQI

We suggest that you consider six steps before implementing CQI in your golf or country club. These are listed below with a brief summary. This book will devote a chapter to each step.

1) Educate the Management

Senior management must acquire a shared appreciation and understanding of Continuous Quality Improvement (CQI) concepts. This can be done in the course of a three-day retreat. At the retreat, the CEO/General Manager must show how proposed plans and implementation actions will result in desired quality improvements.

2) Establish the commitment of the management

Senior management must develop a plan to introduce quality improvement concepts to the stakeholders (customers and employees) including an implementation schedule and identification of target audiences.

3) Establish quality awarness

Senior management must develop a comprehensive, progressive training program aimed at educating employees at all levels to support the program.

4. Establish baseline data

One of the main functions of CQI is to show constant improvement in the quality of service and product delivered. Therefore, measurements must be done in all departments to gather baseline data and then repeated at a later time to see if your processes and systems are improving.

5. Set goals

Once the data is gathered, the facility can set improvement goals.

6. Establish a recognition program

The process is enhanced by recognizing employees who develop quality ideas and boost productivity and customer satisfaction. Any recognition ceremony, which probably shouldn't be initiated for two or more years after starting the CQI effort, should include representatives from both inside your club and from major suppliers (persons that provide you with goods and services) and customers (members of the governing board, employees and members) as well as from people outside the club (local politicians, church leaders, etc.). In addition to the staff and management, the CEO should invite managers from other golf and country clubs from the city or region.

Great minds have purposes, others have wishes.
Washington Irving

Educate The Management

*Y*our CEO and top managers must undertake a training program on the principles of CQI before making a concerted effort to apply them throughout the facility. You'll be making major changes; you can't convince your fellow managers to alter their traditional management style if they don't completely understand the process.

Everyone needs to learn the same information—CEO, managers from all units including the head Golf Professional, Superintendent of Grounds, Food and Service, etc. Your governing board should attend a similar workshop.

At minimum, we recommend that the following five topics be included during the three-day retreat. Each topic should include case studies from other facilities that attempted to implement CQI. In the back of this book, you'll find resources listed. In each chapter we'll list the numbers of the resources you can check for additional guidance.

Topic 1:
Approaches to
Continuous Quality Improvement

The purpose of this topic is to introduce the managers to the approaches of CQI by reviewing the ideas of quality leaders and discussing how their ideas might apply to your club and its mission. We suggest that you discuss philosophies developed by Crosby, Deming, Juran, and Imai. See readings 4, 6, 8, 9, 10, 12, 13, 14, 16, 17, and 18.

Topic 2:
Principles of
Continuous Quality Improvement

The purpose of this topic is to examine the common elements introduced by the various quality experts and discuss how they might be applied to your club and its mission. The common elements that should be discussed are:

1) processes and systems,
2) teaming,
3) customers and suppliers,
4) quality by fact, of process, and by perception,
5) management by fact,
6) complexity, and
7) variation.

See resources 4, 5, and 6.

Topic 3:
Applying the
Malcolm Baldrige Criteria
to Measure Quality

The purpose of this topic is to discuss the nationally recognized procedure encapsulated in the Malcolm Baldrige National Quality Award (MBNQA) Criteria to measure the quality of your facility and its mission. The MBNQA Criteria creates quality standards that provide a target for any service organization. It includes the following categories:

1) leadership,
2) information and analysis,
3) strategic and operational planning,
4) human resource development and management,
5) business process management,
6) performance results, and
7) customer focus and customer and stakeholder satisfaction.

See resource 5.

Topic 4:
The Plan-Do-Check-Act Cycle

The purpose of this topic is to introduce the plan-do-check-act (PDCA) cycle, a fundamental CQI process. Training and discussions should be conducted on:

1) how to identify problems contributing to non value-added work,
2) how to construct effective teams,
3) how to pinpoint the root causes of problems rather than symptoms, and
4) procedures for implementing suggested improvements generated by your teams.

See resource 6.

Action to be effective must be directed to clearly conceived needs. Jawaharial Nehry

Topic 5:
Continuous Quality Improvement
Tools and Techniques

The purpose of this topic is to explain the CQI tools and techniques commonly used to assess the quality of your processes and systems. Eventually, these tools will be used by the quality improvement teams to identify root causes of problems and to make recommendations for improvements. In time, your managers should be able to use and/or understand the following tools:

1) affinity diagram,
2) cause-and-effect diagram,
3) control charts,
4) flow charts,
5) histograms,
6) nominal group process,
7) operational definition,
8) Pareto Diagram,
9) relations diagram,
10) run chart,
11) scatter diagram,
12) scenario builder, and the
13) systematic diagram.

See resources 4 and 6.

At the end of this first step toward implementing quality improvement, you should have managers educated in the philosophy CQI.

Quality is never an accident; it is always the result of high intention, sincere effort, intelligent direction and skillful execution; it represents the wise choice of many alternatives.
Willa A. Foster

If it is going to be practical and achievable, quality management must start at the top.

Philip B. Crosby

Establish
Commitment
of The
Management

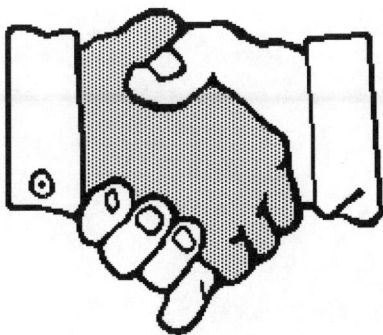

CHAPTER TWO

ow it's time for the CEO and top managers to introduce CQI concepts— including an implementation schedule and identification of target audiences— to the members and employees of your club. Managers must do much more than make an announcement that the golf club will be converting to a quality philosophy. Your CEO must work with the senior managers to accomplish the following understandings:

Make it apparent that CQI is not being tested as a concept

Employees must know that CQI is being implemented throughout the entire facility. As pointed out by Peters and Austin in *A Passion for Excellence* (1985), *[a]ttention to quality can become the organization's mind-set only if **all** of its managers—indeed, all of its people—live it.* They stress that to "live it" means paying attention to quality 100 percent of the time and not allowing occasional lapses.

Appoint a Coordinator for Continuous Quality Improvement

Large golf resorts and country clubs should appoint a Coordinator for CQI. This step is not necessary for regular golf and country clubs as it is more cost effective to employ the services of a consultant to provide an annual workshop for the managers, members of the board, and the employees.

CEO's from large resorts usually think the first step their facility should take is to hire a CQI Coordinator. You may want to rethink that. Why? Because the CQI Coordinator post has become isolated, often filled with individuals with the wrong kind of background. That's definitely a recipe for anything but quality.

After all, at this stage, your facility probably does not have a corporate policy on quality. Without the active support of stakeholders, especially your governing board, the CQI Coordinator can do little to influence the cultural change that is necessary to undertake the transformation to a better quality organization. The end result is that neither quality nor the CQI Coordinator is perceived as really being important.

Many CQI Coordinators quickly become irrelevant for another reason: they have been trained in an industrial setting and know next to nothing about the operation of a golf facility or country club. They do know how to facilitate functional and cross-functional teams and how to use a variety of CQI tools and techniques, but understand little about the processes and systems in the golf facilities. That often creates a chasm between the Coordinator and the managers that no quality plan can bridge.

In addition, the Coordinator position itself may even have a detrimental affect on work morale. Staff, who should have the responsibility of evaluating quality, may start seeing the person who holds the Coordinator title not as a partner or facilitator, but rather as a judge. As a result, the CQI Coordinator often ends up not only managing by fact, but also becoming a behaviorist who must overcome fears, appease egos and continually recognize the accomplishments of people, especially middle managers.

How many coordinators have sufficient training for that complex role?

Still, some of you will need someone to head your facilities quality effort, especially with the ever increasing societal demand that demands improved quality standards.

The Coordinator for CQI should have extensive experience in quality management as well as with golf and country clubs. We caution the CEO to be extremely careful about employing a Continuous Quality Improvement "expert" from industry who does not have considerable experience in the golfing industry since the industry has many unique organizational problems not found in either manufacturing or other service industries. We recommend that s/he be totally familiar with the principles and procedures of CQI, and the job description include the following duties:

- Develop and teach quality awareness programs for all personnel.

- Constantly survey the employees as to task, process, and system problems requiring improvement.

- Educate the CQI quality advisory councils (see below) appointed by the CEO as well as the community advisory council, and members of the governing board.

- Promote the customer/supplier concept throughout the club.

- Meet with external "customers" to understand their perceptions of the club.

- Encourage the integration of process and system designs with emphasis on error-free processes.

- Recommend the allocation of resources to properly meet process and system requirements.

- Establish detection methods that point out process and system errors.

- Establish benchmarking and statistical techniques for the various departments.

- Coordinate the development of the club's long-term strategy towards CQI.

- Publish a newsletter that communicates CQI successes (and failures).

- Post graphs and charts showing CQI trends for various departments.

- Manage the CQI center as described below.

Appoint a CQI
community advisory council

The CEO will need the assistance of a CQI advisory council, comprised of **suppliers** (vendors supplying you with products and services) and **customers** (such as members and employees). We recommend that the CQI advisory council receive the same training as described in Chapter One, either at the same time the upper management does, or with training sessions designed specifically for them.

The training is important because it reduces barriers and provides the necessary background in CQI ideas. By bringing the external groups with their varying perspectives together, the council not only acts as a barometer of public opinion about your facility, but also provides valuable information as how better to guide your facility's CQI efforts.

He that won't
be counselled
can't be helped.
Benjamin Franklin

Appoint a CQI advisory council for each unit/department

Appointing a CQI advisory council for each unit/ department is reserved usually for large resorts and country clubs and is not necessary for average size facilities. In large resorts we recommend creating a separate CQI advisory council for each functional area, *e.g.*, Food & Beverage. It should consist of professionals from the community, the department manager, several members, and several unit employees. Councils should be expected to hold regular meetings that are devoted entirely to CQI and should be required to report quarterly on their achievements to the Coordinator for CQI (or the CEO). Quality meetings should be as important as any other departmental gathering.

These CQI councils should be expected to:

1. Focus the unit's quality processes towards desired objectives that are consistent with the club's mission and long-range goals.

2. Ensure that the CQI education is adequate and ongoing.

3. Do continual reviews and benchmarking and display quality-improvement trends in forms of graphs and charts.

4. Use CQI procedures to constantly prioritize and update those tasks, processes, and systems that appear to be adding to the cost of nonquality.

5. Encourage participation of all employees in quality-improvement teams.

6. Recognize quality improvements internally and externally.

7. Identify and correct tasks, processes, and systems that detract from a quality service or product.

It takes nearly as much ability to know how to profit by good advice as to know how to act for one's self.
Francois de La Rochefoucauld

Encourage members of the governing board to undergo CQI training

You can't overlook the governing board. Members will need to attend an in-depth training session at least once a year as most members come from the traditional business settings which do not really practice CQI. They need to understand and appreciate CQI reports and terminology.

Once the board members become convinced of the value of CQI, they will serve as ardent supporters of your CQI efforts and as such become advocates with the community. This support should lead to increased customer satisfaction.

Finally, after CQI is implemented, board members will very likely insist that future CEO's and managers completely understand CQI and are committed to it. Since members of the governing board usually serve as a link between the club and the customers, they could be instrumental in getting everyone involved in the transformation to quality.

Education is a progressive discovery of our ignorance.
Will Durant

Have a management team write a quality philosophy guide book

After the CEO and the governing board have established a vision statement of what they would like their facility to be within the next decade, the CEO and top management should write a quality philosophy handbook. (For large resorts and large country clubs this project should be coordinated by the Coordinator for CQI as a continuous "work-in-progress.") It gives employees a text which they can refer to and revise, and provides an important sense of participation rather than being subject to a process.

The importance of this guidebook should not be underestimated. It should clearly and succinctly state the club's mission and the importance of quality in delivering high quality experiences.

**Quality improvement has no chance unless the individuals are ready to recognize that improvement is necessary.
Philip B. Crosby**

Make quality improvement an agenda item at performance evaluations

Crosby (1984) states that after the CQI policy has been instituted, usable status reports have to be part of important meetings. To fulfill that guideline, you will need to maintain constant performance evaluations based on quality concepts and make quality a regular part of meetings between the CEO and the senior managers. They should maintain a close watch on the following:

1)   *The quality improvement process*
   - *How many employees have been educated?*
   - *Are the teams functioning properly?*
   - *What success stories do we have to share?*
   - *What problems need action?*

2)   *The cost of quality*
   - *Do we have the format in all operations?*
   - *What are the trends?*
   - *Where do the biggest improvement opportunities lie?*
   - *What problems need action?*

3)   *Conformance*
   - *Are we meeting our requirements?*
   - *What actions do we have to take to emphasize the need to meet them?*

Establish and measure quality goals

Your club will have to review constantly its progress regarding *the quality improvement process, the cost of quality, and its conformance toward meeting goals.* To achieve this end, we suggest that the management be trained in Hoshin Planning.

It is obvious that progress towards CQI must begin with the support of the CEO and the top management since they control the allocation of resources. If they set an example for the rest of the club, middle managers and their employees will quickly recognize that the movement is authentic and not just the latest fad. The managers and staff will eventually accept the fact that the CQI movements are not just another method to increase productivity but a very real commitment towards **quality**.

That doesn't mean managers and staff may not feel threatened by the CQI effort. That can be overcome by establishing trust outside some artificial time commitment. It will take time to create that trust and to develop pride-in-workmanship and an increase in quality. Eventually, though, a new culture will be established, too.

See resources 3, 7 and 15.

In summary, the first step to implementing CQI in a golf or country club is to educate the management. The second step is to have management take a leadership role in making a firm commitment towards CQI.

When it's a pleasure to come to work because the requirements for quality are taken seriously and management is helpful, then attitudes change permanently. Philip B. Crosby

CHAPTER THREE

Establish Quality Awareness

W e believe that quality awareness is best approached by first educating the employees about the principles of CQI techniques and then have them use their training to take corrective action, remove causes of errors in processes and systems, and participate in quality councils and teams.

Educate the employees

Critical to the success of CQI is the education of general managers along with managers and staff. Once the managers and staff understand the principles of CQI, they will commit to the movement even if only in incremental amounts. The education of managers and staff should include an understanding of:

1) teaming,
2) quality philosophies and processes, as well as training in the
3) Plan-Do-Check-Act or P-D-C-A cycle and on the
4) tools and techniques that they will need in order to implement CQI.

It will be necessary to separate the various departments and to tailor the programs for each unit, such as the pro shop, the accounting department, food & beverage, building and grounds, etc.

The obvious reason for educating the employees on CQI is to inform them that their participation is essential for the processes to work. After they realize that their contributions are respected and their responsibilities for improving the quality are essential, most employees will make the commitment. If, after they receive training, employees return to the job and discover that they cannot change systems and processes because they do not have the necessary resources or support to implement what they have learned, the CQI movement will fail as the frustration level increases.

Crosby states (1984, p. 111) that quality has to become part of the corporate culture. Everyone should understand that management is committed to quality, and, therefore, quality is the policy. He emphasizes that the employees must be informed on the cost of not doing a task correctly the first time. (What are the real costs to your club when you cannot retain a member?)

You cannot expect anyone to do anything for which they have not been educated or trained to do.
Robert A. Cornesky

Establish quality councils

Crosby (1984) points out that *[t]he idea of quality councils is to bring the quality professionals together and let them learn from each other* (p. 119). This is an excellent way in which to keep the organization focused on "quality" issues and to prevent slippage back to the traditional manner of operation. "Quality councils" is truly a necessity to ensure that the club's subcultures are pointed in the same direction since many managers and employees often believe that CQI programs are not really applicable to their units.

The only thing to do with good advice is to pass it on.
Oscar Wilde

Establish quality improvement teams

Forming effective improvement teams is central to CQI. A main purpose of improvement teams is to identify problems and then to take the corrective actions necessary to eliminate their reoccurrence. Corrective action does not consist of redoing someone else's mistakes but may involve identifying suppliers who are not meeting conformance standards and then communicating precisely what you expect from their product or service. The supplier might be external such as the supplier of your insecticide, or internal such as the Food & Beverage Department.

In order to get everyone involved in adopting the new quality philosophy, Crosby (1984, p. 106) clearly states that the organization must form quality improvement teams (QIT), consisting of individuals who represent all functions of the organization. The QIT's are more than inter-disciplinary committees. In golf and country clubs **cross-functional teams** are rare: it is uncommon to place secretaries, custodial personnel, pro shop personnel, building and grounds personnel, and the CEO on a team to do anything. One can only speculate what would happen at most clubs if such teams were established routinely in order to implement a continuous quality improvement culture.

Crosby says the CQI team should:

1)   have clear directions for its purpose to guide, coordinate, and support the entire quality implementation process;

2)   have power to clear obstacles and to commit resources;

3)   primarily be concerned with setting up of educational activities; and that

4)   the chairperson of the team should have direct and easy access to the CEO.

We recommend that all managers be a part of quality improvement teams if for no other reason than the activity will constantly remind them of the importance of the quality effort to identify poor systems and to take corrective action steps. This should result in people concentrating on improving poor tasks, processes, and systems and less on blaming and finger pointing.

The second step in the quality improvement effort combines the interrelationship between using the education acquired in the first two steps with **teaming** in order to identify poor **processes and systems** prior to taking corrective action. Let's examine the principles of teaming and processes and systems.

Teaming

Teams and teamwork are extremely important in the process of producing a quality service or product. Although hierarchy is needed within all organizations to avoid chaos, most work in golf and country clubs is accomplished across, not within, organizational boundaries.

According to Hrebiniak (1978, p. 137):

> *. . . in organizations with strong hierarchical and status differences, communications will be vertical in nature, and often biased. Top-level personnel make important decisions and lower-level personnel implement them. This results in a predominantly up-down flow of task-related information. The respect for people of higher status may result in a reluctance to criticize their ideas, and cause the transmission of information that subordinates feel superiors would like to hear.*
>
> *The emphasis on vertical communications further suggests that the tall pyramidal organization performs best when tasks are not very complex and most activity involves simple coordination. . . . However, when problems are complex, individuals may be overwhelmed by the quantity of information. . . . Thus, for nonroutine, complex matters, the prognosis for effective problem solving in the hierarchical system does not appear to be a good one.*

The informal power structure and the resulting culture in golf and country clubs do not readily permit collegiality in a management system based upon hierarchy; however, teaming, when done properly, is invariably found in golf and country clubs having high morale.

In their recent books, Waterman (1990) and Levering (1988) stress the importance of teamwork in effecting change and in keeping morale high.

An excellent way of helping people to embrace change is to identify the causes that detract from doing quality work. This may be done by using one or more of the tools listed in the following table.

See resources 4 and 6.

SEVERAL EXTREMELY USEFUL
CONTINUOUS QUALITY IMPROVEMENT TOOLS THAT CAN BE USED
TO IDENTIFY AND RANK
"PROCESSES" AND/OR "SYSTEMS" PROBLEMS.

Affinity Diagram
- Used to examine complex and/or hard to understand problems
- Used to build team consensus
- Results can be further analyzed by a **Relations Diagram**

Cause and Effect Diagram (Fishbones)
- Used to identify **root causes** of a problem
- Used to draw out many ideas and/or opinions about the causes

Flow Charts
- Gives a picture of the process and the system

Force Field Analysis
- Used when changing the system might be difficult and/or complex

Histogram
- A bar graph of data which displays information about the data set and shape
- Can be used to predict the stability in the system

Nominal Group Process
- A structured process to help groups make decisions
- Useful in choosing a problem to work on
- Used to build team consensus
- Used to draw out many ideas and/or opinions about the causes

Pareto Diagram
- Bar chart that ranks data by categories
- Used to show that a few items contribute greatly to the overall problem
- Helps the team identify which processes/systems to direct their efforts

Relations Diagram
- Helps the team to analyze the cause and effect relationships between factors
- Directs the team to the **root** causes of a problem

Systematic Diagram
- Used when a broad task or goal becomes the focus of the team's work
- Often used after an **Affinity Diagram** and/or **Relations Diagram**
- Used when the action plan is needed to accomplish the goal

Once a problem has been identified and a quality improvement team established, the team must gather and analyze data from the processes and systems contributing to the perceived problem. After suggestions are recommended and implemented to rectify the problem, the processes and systems are standardized, evaluated, and plans for continuous improvement are implemented. This process is commonly known as the Plan-Do-Check-Act (PDCA) Cycle.

One effective way of getting input about the causes of identified problems in your processes and systems is to post **cause-and-effect** diagrams, known also as fishbone charts and Ishikawa Diagrams. Since most problems have more than one cause, the cause-and-effect diagram is useful in showing the relationships between a problem and multiple causes. They are most effective if the employees who contributed to the initial identification of a problem are asked for their opinion of the causes. The four common main causes of a problem are equipment, procedures, materials, and personnel; however, don't limit the primary categories to only these four categories.

**The world hates change,
yet it is the only thing
that has brought progress.
Charles F. Kettering**

The following figure shows a cause-and-effect diagram with an undesirable, identified problem needing to be resolved. Called an "effect," it could have been identified by one or more of the tools listed above such as the affinity diagram, relations diagram, and/or the nominal group process. As can be seen, the effect can have not only one or more main causes, but also be the result of causes at several levels.

A cause-and-effect diagram showing the various causes of a problem.

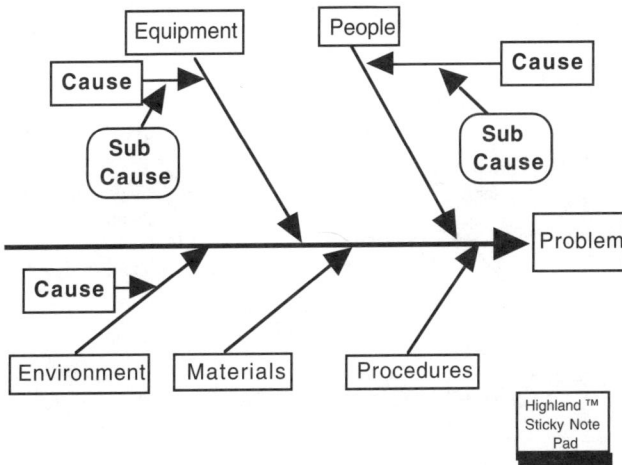

It's a good idea to have a 3 x 4 foot diagram in each management office area when trying to clarify the perceptions about various problems. The sign should have **Highland**™ note pads attached so that the written remarks could be added by the associates, secretaries, members, employees, and anyone else who enters the office. At the end of several weeks, the manager should gather the information and share it, possibly via a newsletter.

Below is a **cause-and-effect** diagram showing the factors as perceived by the employees and the customers related to the loss of sales of the Food & Beverage (F&B) service at their country club.

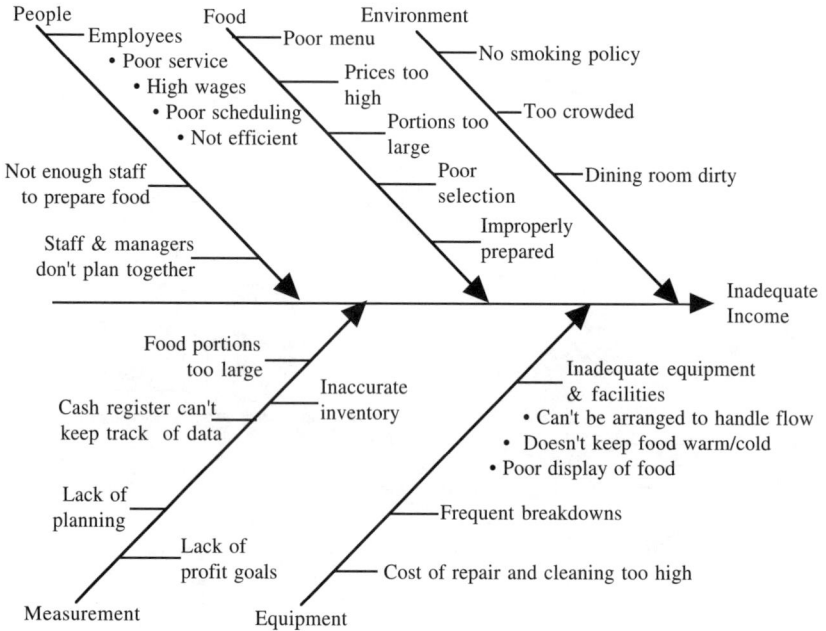

Processes and Systems

Many quality leaders stress improving the processes and systems in which employees work in order to improve the quality of goods and services. Deming and Juran stress that since management controls at least 85 percent of the processes and systems, the majority of poor quality results is due to poor management emphasizing results alone rather than improving processes.

Every work activity is a part of a process and system, and there are countless processes and systems that exist in every department of your club. If golf and country clubs work through processes and systems, it follows that they can improve only if they improve the processes and systems in which the employees work. It also follows that if managers at golf and country clubs improve the processes and systems, they will not only get better quality results but they will increase productivity as well.

A "system" as used in this text is an arrangement of persons, places, things, and/or circumstances that either makes, facilitates, or permits things to happen. The very nature of a system will determine what will happen and how it will happen.

Since most CEO's inherit organizations established by previous managers, they face the challenge of maintaining the strengths and eliminating the weaknesses of existing systems. Since managers control 85-90 percent of the processes and systems, we are convinced that if they seriously commit to quality, they can influence the workforce to do likewise. Employees will most likely work hard if they are convinced that quality will be the end result. If management directs all of its energies towards improving the processes and systems for quality results with, of course, those responsible for providing and receiving the service, we are confident that quality results will end in a modified behavior, a better attitude and eventually an organizational culture directed towards achieving quality.

The measurement of quality is the price of nonconformance. Philip B. Crosby

In summary, the first step to implementing CQI in a golf or country club is to educate the management. The second step is to have management take a leadership role in making a firm commitment towards CQI. The third step is to establish quality awareness throughout the facility by having the employees educated in CQI, establishing quality advisory councils and quality improvement teams.

We cannot direct the wind... but we can adjust the sails.
Anonymous

*Establish
Baseline
Data*

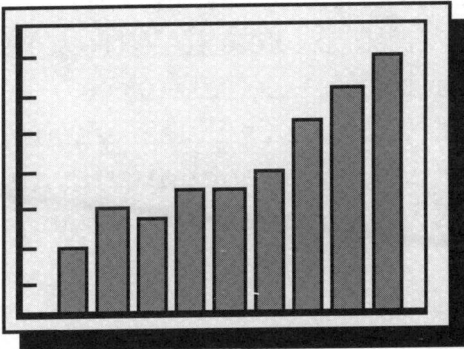

CHAPTER FOUR

*C*rosby makes the point that gathering baseline data is necessary for evaluating the improvement process. He states that people become frustrated when such data are not available and, as a result, they don't know how they are doing. In fact, he implies that people and organizations become frustrated when they do not have clear performance measurements.

Since one of the main functions of CQI is to show constant improvement in the quality of service and product delivered, measurements must be done in all departments in order to gather baseline data and to assess various operations over time to show that the processes and systems are improving.

Gathering data and pointing out defects initially will be considered a threat by employees—but this is a natural response. The only way to overcome that is to establish trust. In golf and country clubs having poor records of cooperation, this may take time. Don't set an artificial deadline; trust requires a long-term relationship (see resources 7 and 15). When trust exists, your staff will feel empowered— they have greater control of not only the functions of their job but also can make their jobs more efficient.

The first way to establish trust is to explain in detail why comprehensive measurements have to be taken. Explanations should show how data can:

1) demonstrate trends in customer satisfaction levels, including their satisfaction with the management and other departments/units;

2) determine if the club is meeting its mission and quality goals;

3) reveal to the customers that the club is improving in efficiency and productivity; and

4) let the employees know how well they and their unit/department is doing.

People perform to the standards of their leaders. If management thinks people don't care then they won't care.
Philip B. Crosby

Second, the employees should also be informed that most of the measurements will be done by their department/unit and will be relevant to their needs as well as the needs of their customers. They should also be informed that the measurements will be simple, understandable, and few in number. The measurements will be done by all departments and divisions, beginning with top management (if not previously done). Because gathering baseline data is valuable as a means of taking a picture of the system, it must include all parts of the organization.

Third, the employees must see that management is committed to quality. Managers must participate in the same kinds of self-examination required of employees. They must be involved in measuring their own effectiveness and making honest judgments from the data.

Fourth, employees will see how the data is used to identify processes and procedures that could be done better and more efficiently. These suggestions are turned over to quality improvement teams and action-oriented task forces to develop corrective action.

Another benefit of combining corrective action with empowerment and trust is that employees feel encouraged to conduct self-directed assessment and to constantly improve their job performance so that things can be done quicker, better and less expensively.

If Conger and Kanungo's (1988) definition of empowerment is accepted as

> . . . *a process of enhancing feelings of self-efficacy among organizational members through the identification of conditions that foster powerlessness and through their removal by both formal organizational practices and informal techniques of providing efficacy information, ...*

then you can extend the trust approach to the level of the individual. Trust and empowerment, therefore, are more than participative management; they are directly involved in self-leadership skill development where one makes decisions and takes action on the best way to solve a problem—especially problems associated with their job. If people feel powerless, on the other hand, they will do as little as possible to maintain their job. Quality will be valued to the lowest common denominator.

Involve everyone and keep it simple

Gather data? That sounds simple enough. It should be, but you may find some objections. Many managers at golf clubs claim that much of what they do is not measurable. That's not accurate. After all, virtually every golf and country club conducts annual evaluations, although they are, for the most part, statistically invalid. Besides, if the processes and systems that managers control cannot be measured, then how are managers to know when they improved a system? The purpose of measuring is not to inspect or to cause fear, but to point out dysfunctional processes and systems that can be improved.

As with managers, the staff are evaluated routinely. Unfortunately, most golf and country clubs use evaluation methods that are not statistically significant and usually end up frightening the employees rather than providing them with an opportunity for improvement. That contradicts the goal of gathering data, which is to provide a standard from which quality can develop.

Get training on
Malcolm Baldrige NationalQuality Award
Criteria

In our book *Quality Index: Self Assessment Rating of Golf and Country Clubs.* (see resource 5), we suggest an evaluation and scoring procedure for determining a **quality index** (QI) for golf and country clubs. We recommended that you evaluate your club's quality by using a modified tool based on the Malcolm Baldrige National Quality Award (MBNQA) Criteria.

The purpose of the QI tool was to suggest an expeditious method to obtain a baseline from which to begin to gather measurement data for a Continuous Quality Improvement program. It should be noted that the suggested method can be used to rate either an entire club, or a single department/unit within the club.

Establish an accounting procedure

Crosby (1984, p. 110) recommends that institutions develop a cost accounting method so all procedures can be consistently measured in the same manner. That's because golf and country clubs often measure costs in entirely different ways. In fact, comparison between golf and country clubs sometimes becomes nearly impossible, even between golf and country clubs owned and operated by the same group. Moreover, data between departments in the same club may be entered and interpreted in different ways.

Quality measurement is effective only when it is done in a manner that produces information that people can understand.
Philip B. Crosby

Collect and plot cost of
non-conformance data

Deming believed that having quotas and numerical goals impedes quality more than any other single working condition. To eliminate quotas and numerical goals, the leadership must constantly measure cost of quality and the cost of non-conformance (CON). Then, after the data is collected, it should be graphed and placed in areas for everyone to see. Remember, the purpose of determining the CON data and plotting it is not to drive in fear, but to let people know where the club's processes and systems are at the present time and in what direction they are headed.

In Gold I trust,
but everyone else
must bring me data.
Dr. W. Edwards Deming

In summary, the first step to implementing CQI in a golf or country club is to educate the management. The second step is to have management take a leadership role in making a firm commitment towards CQI. The third step is to establish quality awareness throughout the club by having the employees educated in CQI, establishing quality advisory councils and quality improvement teams. The fourth step is to take measurements on all performances, processes, and procedures. Then the methods for measuring the cost of quality have to be standardized and the cost of quality and non-conformance have to be determined for all major processes and systems, and the results should be displayed graphically.

Set
Goals

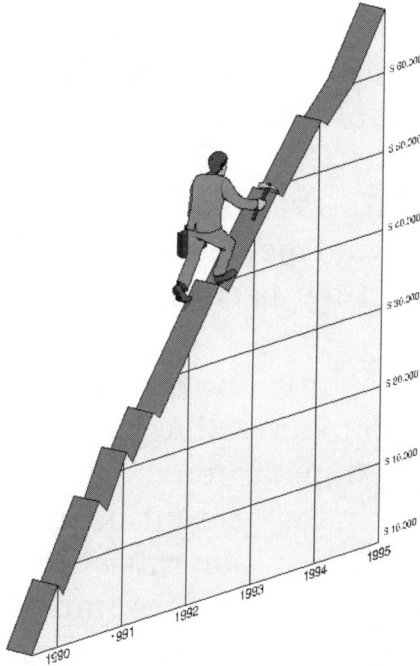

CHAPTER FIVE

Goals are designed to be
measurable and to give
you a clear picture
whether or not you
have achieved them.
Robert A. Cornesky

oal setting, according to Crosby (1984, p. 116), is something that happens when the organization begins to gather data in order to measure improvements. Of course, data is needed by any golf or country club to establish a baseline of performance. Too many golf and country clubs lack sufficient information. Then they don't adequately allocate the funds necessary to implement the plan. As a result, CEO's, managers, board members, staff and members eventually can't determine how well they performed to meet the goals.

We recommend that charts and graphs displaying baseline data as well as projected goals be posted in every department. For example, historical data of member retention rates may demonstrate an annual attrition rate of 15 percent. After better quality procedures are implemented, the club may experience a decrease in the attrition rates over the next three years.

In summary, the first step to implementing CQI in a golf or country club is to educate the management. The second step is to have management take a leadership role in making a firm commitment towards CQI. The third step is to establish quality awareness throughout the club by having the employees educated in CQI, establishing quality advisory councils and quality improvement teams. The fourth step is to take measurements on all performances, processes, and procedures. Then the methods for measuring the cost of quality have to be standardized and the cost of quality and non-conformance have to be determined for all major processes and systems, and the results should be displayed graphically. The fifth step is to define unit, department, and organizational goals based on the data collected then to have the quality improvement teams take corrective action steps in removing causes of errors in processes and systems.

Good things happen only when planned; bad things happen on their own.
Philip B. Crosby

People seldom improve when they have no other model but themselves to copy after.

Goldsmith

Establish
A
Recognition
Program

CHAPTER SIX

*I*nstituting a recognition day could take considerable time. It might take more than two years or so after the quality processes are instituted. In the planning for the recognition day we suggest that representatives from major suppliers and customers as well as from people outside the club be included. In addition to the managers, staff, and members, the CEO should invite managers from other clubs.

Both Crosby (1984, p. 119) and Deming believe that merit pay is a very bad form of recognition. Crosby, however, believes that a serious recognition program for good employees should be created since it is a very important part of the quality movement. Crosby did his recognition awards at an annual black-tie picnic.

We believe that merit pay is an inexpensive way of getting everyone in the club mad at each other. On the other hand, we believe that recognizing individuals and groups for efforts in establishing and/or improving quality should be done annually.

In summary, the first step to implementing CQI in a golf or country club is to educate the management. The second step is to have management take a leadership role in making a firm commitment towards CQI. The third step is to establish quality awareness throughout the club by having the employees educated in CQI, establishing quality advisory councils and quality improvement teams. The fourth step is to take measurements on all performances, processes, and procedures. Then the methods for measuring the cost of quality have to be standardized and the cost of quality and non-conformance have to be determined for all major processes and systems, and the results should be displayed graphically. The fifth step is to define unit, department, and organizational goals based on the data collected then to have the quality improvement teams take corrective action steps in removing causes of errors in processes and systems. The sixth step is to recognize those individuals, teams and units/ departments that have done an outstanding job in identifying process problems and in taking corrective action(s) to eliminate their occurrences. The final step is to do it over again, and again.....

> **Relationships
> are where it all comes
> together or comes apart.
> Nothing else
> can be made to happen
> if relationships
> do not exist.**
>   **Philip B. Crosby**

SUGGESTED READINGS

SUGGESTED READINGS

1. Barker, Joel. *Future Edge: Discovering the New Paradigms of Success.* NY: Wm. Morrow & Co., Inc., 1992.

2. Boedecker, Ray F., *Eleven Conditions for Excellence: The IBM Total Quality Improvement Process.* Boston: American Institute of Management, 1989.

3. Conger, Jay and Rabindra Kanungo.*The Empowerment Process: Integrating Theory and Practice.* Academy of Management Review, July 1988.

4. Cornesky, Andrew R. and Robert A. Cornesky. *Total Quality Management in Golf and Country Clubs.* Port Orange, FL: Cornesky & Associates, Inc. 1993.

5. Cornesky, Andrew R. and Robert A. Cornesky. *Quality Index: Self Assessment Rating of Golf and Country Clubs.* Port Orange, FL: Cornesky & Associates, Inc. 1995.

6. Cornesky, Andrew R. and Robert A. Cornesky. *Continuous Quality Improvement Guide for Golf and Country Club Managers: The Tools and Techniques.* Port Orange, FL: Cornesky & Associates, Inc. 1995.

SUGGESTED READINGS

7. Covey, Stephen R. *The 7 Habits of Highly Effective People*. NY: Simon & Schuster, 1989.

8. Crosby, Philip B. *Quality Without Tears: The Art of Hassle-Free Management*. New York: McGraw-Hill Book Co., 1984.

9. Crosby, Philip B. *Let's Talk Quality*. New York: McGraw-Hill Book Co., 1989.

10. Deming, W. Edwards. *Out of the Crisis*. Cambridge, MA: Productivity Press or Washington, DC: The George Washington University, MIT-CAES, 1982.

11. Hrebiniak, Lawrence G. *Complex Organizations*. New York: West Publishing Co., 1978.

12. Imai, Masaaki. *Kaizen: The Key to Japan's Competitive Success*. Cambridge, MA: Productivity Press, 1986.

13. Ishikawa, Kaoru. *Guide to Quality Control*. Englewood Cliffs, NJ: Prentice Hall, 1982.

14. Juran, J.M. *Juran On Planning For Quality*. Cambridge, MA: Productivity Press, 1988.

SUGGESTED READINGS

15. Levering, Robert. *A Great Place to Work*. New York: Random House, Inc., 1988.

16. Peters, Tom and Nancy Austin. *A Passion for Excellence* . New York: Random House, Inc., 1985.

17. Peters, Tom. *Thriving on Chaos*. New York: Harper & Row, 1988.

18. Waterman, Robert H. *Adhocracy: The Power to Change*. Knoxville, TN: Whittle Direct Books, 1990.

For more information on the following publications, or to order contact:

CORNESKY & ASSOCIATES, INC.
489 Oakland Park Blvd.
Port Orange, FL 32127-9538

PHONE:

(800) 388-8682
or
(904) 760-5866

FAX:

(904) 756-6755

E-MAIL:

TQM1BOB@AOL.COM

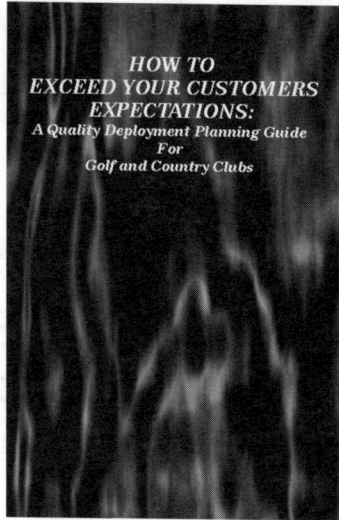

HOW TO EXCEED YOUR CUSTOMERS EXPECTATIONS:
A Quality Deployment Planning Guide For Golf and Country Clubs

This book provides a step-by-step description on how to deploy a quality method and procedure in response to the voice of your customers—your customer's wants, needs and expectations. The authors demonstrate how you can significantly improve your customer satisfaction and loyalty. They take the reader through each stage on the planning and implementation stages of the process, from collection of the customers' voice to the deployment of the critical processes.

The method described in this book provides an organized, practical, and useful procedure to translate what your customers want into practical action-oriented steps at improving their satisfaction through customer-oriented product and services. For many golf and country clubs threatened by competition, this book on customer satisfaction is necessary for survival. *How To Exceed Your Customers Expectations: A Quality Deployment Planning Guide For Golf and Country Clubs* will help you to increase the competitiveness of your club and to develop a base of very satisfied customers.

Cost $29, S&H included • 1st printing January 1997 • 70 pages • ISBN 1-881807-15-0

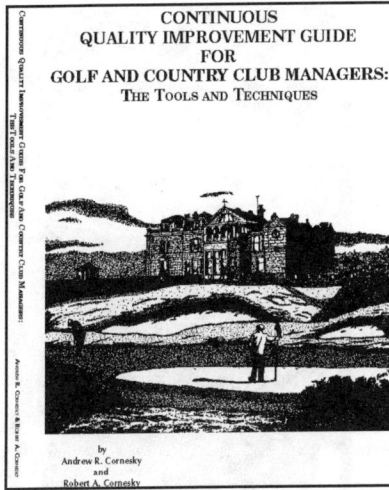

CONTINUOUS
QUALITY IMPROVEMENT GUIDE
FOR
GOLF AND COUNTRY CLUB MANAGERS:
THE TOOLS AND TECHNIQUES

by
Andrew R. Cornesky
and
Robert A. Cornesky

CONTINUOUS QUALITY IMPROVEMENT GUIDE FOR GOLF AND COUNTRY CLUB MANAGERS: THE TOOLS AND TECHNIQUES

The purpose of this manual is to describe a **cooperative model** for CQI which will permit managers to evaluate the quality of their units and club and then by using the described tools and techniques to improve the quality of service and increase customer satisfaction. This manual is for managers of golf and country clubs. It is divided into three chapters. In the first chapter, we present the commonalties in the approaches and principles to continuous quality improvement (CQI). In the second, we present our version of self assessment quality profile index tool based on the Malcolm Baldrige National Quality Award Criteria. This self-assessment should provide you with information that you need on where your various units should most likely begin their quality journey. The third chapter describes the cooperative model. It shows how you can define the quality problems of your club, gives you some pointers on how to establish quality improvement teams (QIT), and walks you through the steps that have to be taken to conduct the improvement study and to recommend solutions to your quality problems. The appendix describes many CQI tools and techniques that you will find invaluable in your quality journey.

Cost: $39, S&H included • 1st printing September 1995 • 150 pages • ISBN 1-881807-11-8.

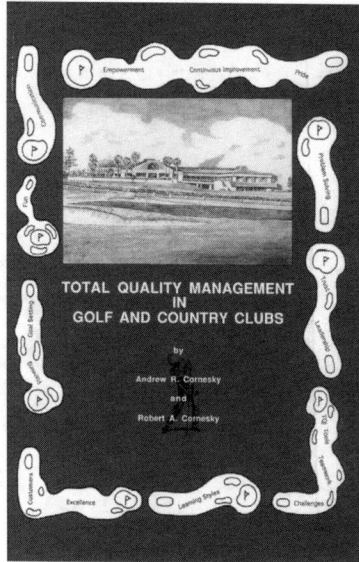

TOTAL QUALITY MANAGEMENT
IN
GOLF AND COUNTRY CLUBS

by

Andrew R. Cornesky
and
Robert A. Cornesky

TOTAL QUALITY MANAGEMENT IN GOLF AND COUNTRY CLUBS

This book makes recommendations on how total quality management (TQM) and total quality improvement (TQI) can be applied to various operations of the golf and country clubs. The primary focus is to help golf clubs increase the quality of their service, decrease costs and encourage additional people, including families, to take up the game for recreation and health. The book begins with an introduction to the approaches of four quality experts, namely, W. Edwards Deming, Joseph Juran, Philip Crosby, and Masaaki Imai. Unlike other books that generally describe how TQM and TQI can be applied to the service industries, we focus on how the approaches can be applied to the golf club. The second chapter compares the commonalties in the principles of the quality gurus. In Chapter Three we took the Malcolm Baldrige Award Criteria and modified them slightly to more nearly fit into the golf club. Then in Chapters Four—10 we examine in greater detail each of the seven award criteria. In Chapter 11 we elaborate on the five conditions that are necessary in your organization, be it the entire country club, the pro shop, or the food and beverage services, to implement TQM. In Chapter 12 we walk the reader through a Plan-Do-Check-Act cycle as we talk about how a quality improvement team can, by using the total quality improvement tools and techniques, actually identify poor processes then implement corrective actions necessary to improve the systems. In Chapter 13 we present our version of a self assessment quality profile index tool based on the modified Malcolm Baldrige Award Criteria. The final chapter describes in detail how some of the total quality improvement tools can help your organization identify problems and improve in quality.

**Cost: $23, S&H included • 1st printing 1993 • 310 pages •
ISBN 1-881807-04-5.**

QUALITY INDEX:
SELF-ASSESSMENT RATING
OF
GOLF AND COUNTRY CLUBS

by
Andrew R. Comesky
and
Robert A. Comesky

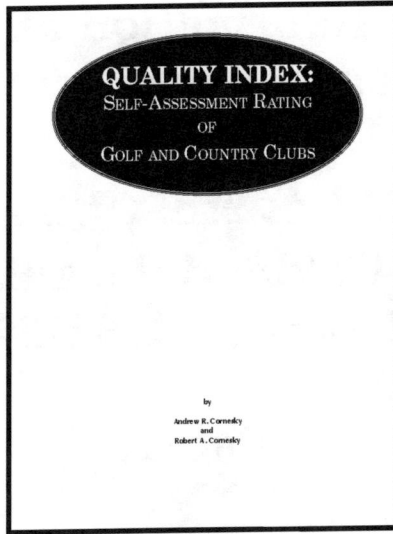

Quality Index: Self-Assessment Rating Instrument for Golf and Country Clubs

This quality index survey instrument is based on the Malcolm Baldrige National Quality Award Criteria (MBNQA). Also included is a Macintosh-based Works™ 3.0 or MSDOS programmed diskette containing the self-scoring instruments. Developed to familiarize managers with the intricacies of the MBNQA Criteria, it measures the quality of golf club processes and systems, and provides a method for determining an approximate quality baseline of golf club services and products before initiating a Continuous Quality Improvement effort. This self-assessment tool has been designed to facilitate the measurement of quality service and product systems. It is not proposed as a mandatory set of guidelines without possibility of modification. The goal is to encourage self-assessment of your golf club's procedures and outcomes. The tool should enable the club managers, governing board members, employees, and customers to grapple with the strong external requirement of golf and county clubs to demonstrate quality and high performance.

Cost: $19, S&H included • 1st printing July 1995 • 18 pages with Diskette • ISBN 1-881807-12-6.

For more information about these publications, or to order contact:

CORNESKY & ASSOCIATES, INC.
489 Oakland Park Blvd.
Port Orange, FL 32127-9538

PHONE:

(800) 388-8682
or
(904) 760-5866

FAX:

(904) 756-6755

E-MAIL:

TQM1BOB@AOL.COM

ABOUT THE AUTHORS

ANDREW R. CORNESKY

Vice President of Research and Development of Cornesky & Associates, Inc., Cornesky is a nationally acclaimed speaker and consultant who was first to demonstrate the applicability of **Total Quality Management** (TQM) to golf and country clubs. A golf professional, and is co-author of three of the best-selling books on TQM in the golf industry, *Total Quality Management in Golf and Country Clubs, Continuous Quality Improvement Guide for Golf and Country Club Managers* and *How To Exceed Your Customers Expectations: A Quality Deployment Planning Guide For Golf and Country Clubs.*

ROBERT A CORNESKY, Sc.D.

Dr. Cornesky, nationally recognized author of eight books and numerous articles on TQM. He was the first person to apply TQM to educational institutions. He was a Senior Examiner for Florida's Sterling Quality Award and founding editor of the *TQM in Higher Education* newsletter. He is now President of Cornesky & Associates, Inc., a nationally known consulting firm specializing in Total Quality Management for service industries and is the editor of *The Chronicle of CQI*.